The Art of Biblical Affirmations: Overcoming chronic illness, chronic pain, depression with God's word and His grace.
Vol. 2
NNylari Iralynn

Tonita Walker * Melanie Hughes

Copyrights

The Art of Biblical Affirmations Vol.2
Copyright @2020 by Iralynn Johnson, NNylari Iralynn. All rights reserved. Printed in the United States of America. No part of this book may be used or reproduced in any manner without written permission except in the case of brief quota in articles, reviews and/or used in art parties or group settings.

Dedication

I dedicate this book to the love of my life, Jesus Christ my Lord and savior, to every person who has experienced some form of chronic pain in their lives, to the person who has or may be experiencing depression, to my handsome sons Jalen, Milan, and Judah. It is my prayer that this book of positive affirming words, images, expressions, and my honest truth will allow you to see and understand a different perspective on how to handle chronic illnesses, chronic pain, depression and how to press through the hard times. Let's overcome together.

I Am who I am because

God's word, music, art, writing, singing, imagining, creating, fashion, and motivating others are my coping skills. I am who I am because of God and the talents He has allowed me to use to inspire His people.

I am NNylari Iralynn, Renaissance woman

The Art of Biblical Affirmations: Overcoming chronic illness, chronic pain, depression with God's word and His grace.
Vol. 2

2 Corinthians 4:17

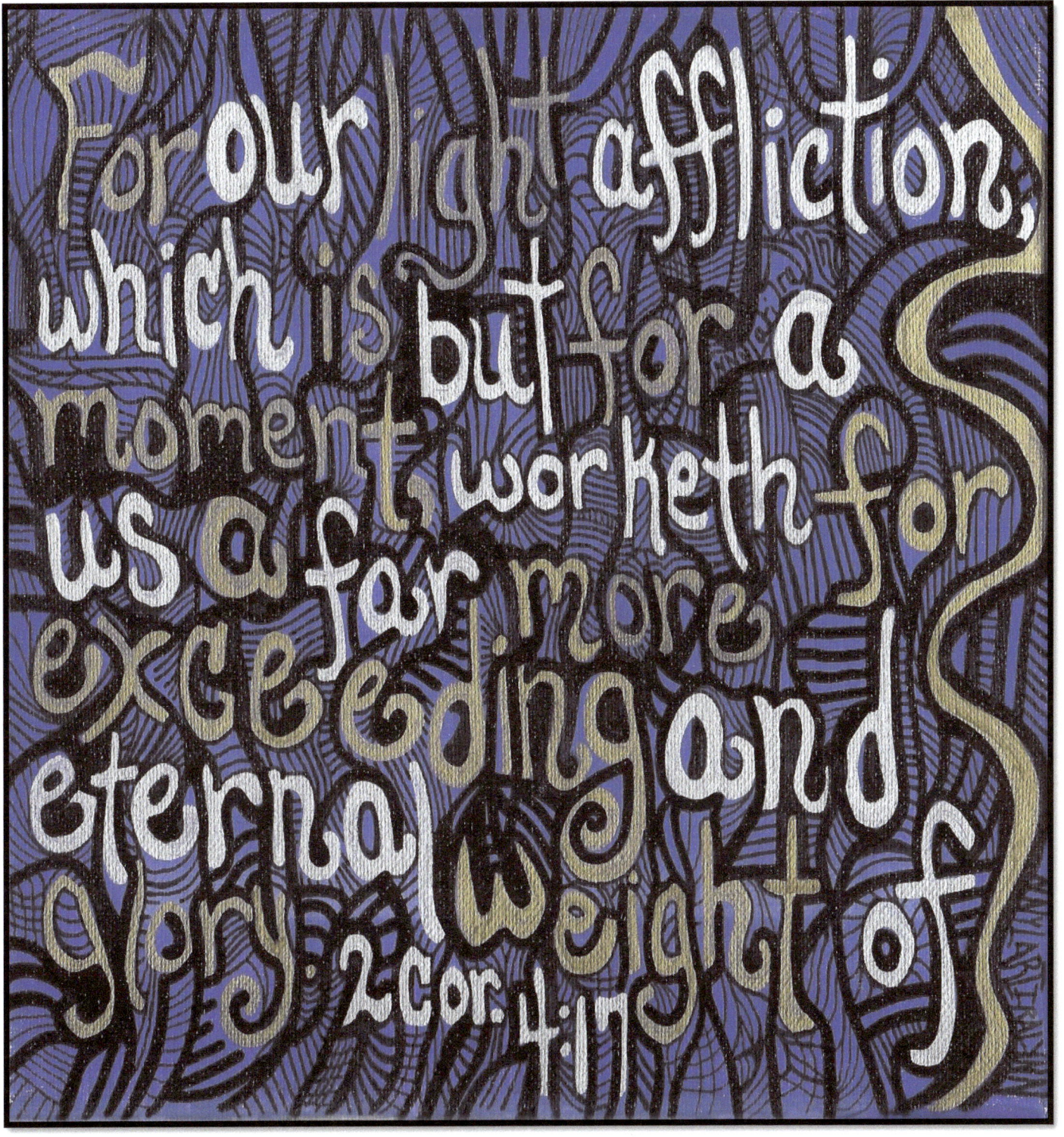

TABLE OF CONTENT

Introduction...9

The Purpose of this Book...10

Gods gives what we don't deserve....................................11

2 Corinthians 12:9...13

Chapter 1: Chronic Illness, Chronic Pain, Depression..........14

The grieving process defined...17

Chapter 2: My Story..26

Chapter 3: I will wait patiently on the Lord......................37

Chapter 4: God will strengthen and help me....................42

Chapter 5: I am not alone..47

Chapter 6: I will put my hope in God................................52

Chapter 7: God will take care of me..................................57

Chapter 8: God's Will Must Be Done.................................62

Introduction

How far do you allow negative thoughts to get in your mind? Part of my struggle with depression is how long I allow the suggested thought to sit on mind. Suggested thoughts happen at any given time because the enemy knows what our weaknesses are, what we have been through and he enjoys planting negative seeds to push us off track. I was a teenager when I realized that I struggled with depression. I knew I loved God but because of many negative experiences such as being molested by one of my female cousins and raped by one of my male cousins, I became depressed. God gifted me with the talent to draw, paint, sing, and write. God, also gave me my best friend and partner, my sister Tonita, and my amazing parents. With these tools I was able to press past the negative thoughts that would so easily creep in my mind. I didn't know it at the time but it was my way to cope with what was taking place in my mind. Because I had a very strong foundation of faith and God's word all my life, I had an unknown shield. Although I didn't know or under what I had, it was there working on my behave. Twenty years later I am more aware of the tools God has given me and I pray that this book of affirmations, God's word, and coloring pages will help you create a new way to combat depression, negative thoughts, and chronic pain.

I am an overcomer of depression. I know that I can make it through anything with the necessary tools. God's word, prayer, music, a pencil, paper, paint, music and positive people are my tools. I will use my tools to keep my mind focused on God's plan and I will not allow my battle ground (My mind) to be invaded by the negativity of depressing thoughts that are suggested by the enemy. I am prepared to destroy every negative thought every time because God has made me an overcomer!

The purpose of this book

The purpose of this book is to help you redirect your focus on God and His word. God wants your attention. God wants you to give all of your problems to him. Open your bible daily to receive what God has for you.

In all honesty we don't spend enough time with God and His word. We are so consumed by the distractions within this world that we forget where our focus should be. We consume our time with television, the newest sitcoms, the news, texting, talking on the phone, shopping for things we don't need, entertaining relationships we have no business being in, gossip, working more than we should because you think more money will solve your problem, and so many other selfish endeavors that we miss the opportunity to grow our relationship with God.

If we stay focused on the solution, we overcome the problem. We can overcome negative thoughts by applying Gods word to it and positivity. Reading, studying, meditating, and applying God's word to our lives will help you overcome. God's word is truth and it will last forever more.

Matthew 24:35 (kjv)
Heaven and earth shall pass away, but my words shall not pass away.

Isaiah 40:8 (kjv)
8 The grass withereth, the flower fadeth: but the word of our God shall stand for ever.

John 2:17 (kjv)
17 And the world passeth away, and the lust thereof: but he that doeth the will of God abideth forever.

Psalm 119:89 (kjv)
89 Forever, O Lord, thy word is settled in heaven

1 Peter 1:25 (kjv)
25 But the word of the Lord endureth forever. And this is the word which by the gospel is preached unto you.

Psalm 12:6-7King James Version (KJV)
6 The words of the Lord are pure words: as silver tried in a furnace of earth, purified seven times.
7 Thou shalt keep them, O Lord, thou shalt preserve them from this generation forever.

Gods gives what we don't deserve

It's amazing how God looks out for us, even when we don't realize it, God is fighting for us. God gave His only son so that we might have a way back to Him, and That's some kind of grace and love that is far past our human understanding. Grace is a wonderful gift that God has given us. Gods loving arms are always open to receive us when we mess up, fall, and do wrong. Grace is Gods way of showing us unmerited favor when we don't deserve it. Every time I tried to end it all, every time I allowed my feelings to get in the way of Gods plan for my life, I could always see God's hand in the situation, reaching out to pull me back up. God's grace is like an extension cord, when you mess up and do wrong (can't reach the plug), God extends His merciful hand (the extension cord) to give us grace to make it through and plug us back in to Him. We have all come short of God's glory but yet God still sees fit to show us grace and mercy. We are here only by God's grace.

Hebrews 4:16 KJV

16 Let us therefore come boldly unto the throne of grace, that we may obtain mercy, and find grace to help in time of need.

1 Peter 1:13 KJV

13 Wherefore gird up the loins of your mind, be sober, and hope to the end for the grace that is to be brought unto you at the revelation of Jesus Christ;

John 1:16-17 KJV
16 And of his fulness have all we received, and grace for grace.

17 For the law was given by Moses, but grace and truth came by Jesus Christ.

2 Corinthians 12:9

And he said unto me, my grace is sufficient for thee: for my strength is made perfect in weakness. Most gladly therefore will I rather glory in my infirmities, that the power of Christ may rest upon me.

Chapter 1

Chronic Illness, Chronic Pain, Depression and the Grieving Process defined

What is a Chronic Illness?

Chronic illness is an uncontrolled disorder and the expiration of that said illness is unknown. If an illness last longer than a year or more, the person is required to see a doctor for ongoing care due to that said illness, it is considered a chronic illness.

Asthma, Degenerative Disc Disease, Crohn Disease, Multiple Sclerosis, Parkinson's Disease, HIV/AIDS, COPD-Chronic Obstructive Pulmonary, Heart Disease, Mood Disorders (Depression, Bipolar Disorder), Diabetes, and Hypertension (high blood pressure) are all common chronic illnesses.

What is Chronic Pain?

There is no specific cure for chronic pain but there are medications, exercises, and procedures that can reduce the level of pain that is experience. Chronic pain is an ongoing feeling that has no set end.

What is Depression?

It is in our lowest moments, when God ministers to our hearts with his Word, it is the perfect intimate time with Him.

Depression is an ongoing feeling of sorrow and a lack of curiosity in the things you once loved or had passion for.

There are many people in the bible who loved God, but we're depressed, hurt, and even overwhelmed with grief. After experiencing many loses in life Job was depressed. (Read Job chapter 1-3, and Job chapter 38-42).

David was also depressed and he was honest about it.

Psalm 69:3-5 NKJV

³ I am weary with my crying;
My throat is dry;
My eyes fail while I wait for my God.

⁴ Those who hate me without a cause
Are more than the hairs of my head;
They are mighty who would destroy me,
Being my enemies wrongfully;
Though I have stolen nothing,
I *still* must restore *it.*

⁵ O God, you know my foolishness;
And my sins are not hidden from You.

The Grieving Process

The grieving process is grieving for people, things or activities you can no longer do or see and embracing what you are still capable of doing and remembering the relationship. This is a very challenging place to be at in life. We experience death on more than one occasion in this life and know how to flow through it and remembering that God has all power to give and take is key.

It's not easy for many of us to drop what has been our norm for decades of our lives and begin anew. Starting over without a person, without that item or without full range of motion in your body can be devastating. This is why we need God to help guide us through our painful loss and show us the roses that remain with us when one rose dies. God shows us how to take the withered rose petals and use them as Potpourri. Sometimes things have to die to push you into your next season in life.

Because everyone is different, a person can spend more time in one area of the grieving process than others. One of the issues we have is the fact that many of us don't realize that we are actually going through the grief process, especially when it's not an actual person that has died. Grief applies to what once was, and that's what must be processed. The process is different in regards to time frame and how its handled for each individual. Some people can grieve for a few months and be okay and others take years to grieve. The most important thing is to go through the process so that you can gain closure and a new start in life. There is a time and season for all things.

Ecclesiastes 3:1-13 KJV

3 To every thing there is a season, and a time to every purpose under the heaven:

2 A time to be born, and a time to die; a time to plant, and a time to pluck up that which is planted;

3 A time to kill, and a time to heal; a time to break down, and a time to build up;

4 A time to weep, and a time to laugh; a time to mourn, and a time to dance;

5 A time to cast away stones, and a time to gather stones together; a time to embrace, and a time to refrain from embracing;

6 A time to get, and a time to lose; a time to keep, and a time to cast away;

7 A time to rend, and a time to sew; a time to keep silence, and a time to speak;

8 A time to love, and a time to hate; a time of war, and a time of peace.

9 What profit hath he that worketh in that wherein he laboureth?

10 I have seen the travail, which God hath given to the sons of men to be exercised in it.

11 He hath made every thing beautiful in his time: also he hath set the world in their heart, so that no man can find out the work that God maketh from the beginning to the end.

12 I know that there is no good in them, but for a man to rejoice, and to do good in his life.

13 And also that every man should eat and drink, and enjoy the good of all his labour, it is the gift of God.

The are 5 stages of grief

1. Denial & Isolation
2. Anger
3. Bargaining
4. Depression
5. Acceptance

1. Denial & Isolation

When someone denies something, they have made up in their mind that it never happened. Denial is something that is short term and it is also used as a defense. These feelings will diminish as days go by, responsibility comes, and different events, situations take place that require the presence of that person or require that entity to be present but can no longer be present because it has died.

Isolation is when you separate, segregate, set apart, quarantine, insulate, shield, or seclude yourself from other people. When someone doesn't understand your feelings and the emotions that come with a loss, it can cause a person to feel alone, and isolated. Isolation can occur during a major shift in life that can consist of the loss of a family member or losing other things that are of value to you.

2. Anger

Hostile, displeasure, irritability, vexation, annoyance, and rage are all words that describe anger. Anger is a very strong intense emotion that is expressed in different ways depending on the person who is angry.
When denial cannot be continued, a person may become angry, and resentful. When someone is angry, they may ask why this is happening to them. Some people take their anger out on other people who are around, causing harm to those relationships and some blame God.

The bible says in Ephesians 4:26 Be ye angry, and sin not: let not the sun go down upon your wrath:

3. Bargaining

God, if you would just give me back my ability to run Marathons, I promise I will do whatever you want me to do. God if you would just give me my mother back, I promise I won't miss church anymore. These are examples of how people bargain with God hoping for a magical change in what has already taken place. A person may feel guilty and think that they could have done things differently and they would have different results. I can remember trying to think of how I did this to my back. Thinking that if I had exercised more and cleaned up my diet that I wouldn't have Degenerative Disc Disease. This is all a part of the grieving process and it's just as challenging as all the other steps so have your bargaining moments but know that there is a brighter side coming and God always has a master plan for all things and every situation. If God took it, or if God allowed it to die, best believe He is birthing a new but it's all in your going through. Don't rush the process.

4. Depression

What many church pastors, preachers and teachers don't tell us is that you can be depressed and still hear from God, be on assignment for God, and have much purpose. Depression doesn't mean that your mind has been consumed with negativity, in fact I would argue that depression is an infection of a section of your thought life that can lead to a takeover if you don't act fast. When I say act fast, I mean, to have something (prayer, bible scriptures, positive words, affirmations, a plan for depressing moments, etc.) in place to counteract the depression. Depression is a normal part of grieving but you just can't pack up your whole house and live there. There has to be a cut off period and some people don't know when to cut it off so they need help in that area. Depression comes before the last step in the grieving process.

5. Acceptance

Acceptance is when you have found the strength to rest in your current circumstance, you're in a different head space, and you're in a place of adaption. Acceptance means that you understand that your loved one is no longer with you, or that you no longer have that ability. You may not be completely okay with losing but you have accepted that life has to change now, you have gained the strength to push through the hard times, and you understand that your life is different and rebuilding is part of moving on. Rebuilding with all the good and bad memories of how things once were is a peace, and comfort for you in this stage.

Are you grieving? Yes or No

If so, who or what died?

What are your thoughts right now?

Notes/Reflections

Notes/Reflections (How did this affirmation and art work make you feel? Write, draw, color your response below.)

Chapter 2
My Story

Tonita Walker's story

In the year of 2015, I woke up, and got dressed to go to a follow-up doctor's appointment. I arrive at the doctor's office thinking to myself... I'm good, just like a regular appointment... clear bill of health. Until the doctor speaks, and says.... Good morning Mrs. Walker, thanks for coming back in so quickly... we got your blood work back, and the results from your physical. The test shows that not only do you have high blood pressure, but you also have type 2 diabetes, and asthma. Really!!! No doctor wait... no not me! I'm sorry Mrs. Walker, but the test is accurate. Oh, this weight is so heavy... my strength is weakened by it! Lord why me? Stress has made its home in me, and Depression walks through the door trying to unpack. Night falls, eyes wide open as I lay in the bed trying to fall asleep but the fear of dying when my eyes close causes sleep to hide from me. I get up, and walk to the bathroom... look in the mirror, and say to myself...NITA what have you done to yourself (tears begin to fill my eyes)! I was beginning to think that life was over for me, and I was the cause of my shortened life. All I could say is... Jesus help me ... I am afraid to go to sleep cause if I do, I won't wake back up again.... Face flooded with tears as I cry soundless to myself and nothing else could be said... So, I dried my tears, and walked back into the room. I lay back in the bed, and attempt to fall asleep again, but still sleep hides from me. Then I hear someone say ..."I'M HEAR"... I look over my left shoulder to see if it was my husband, but he was sound asleep. Once again, I hear someone say "I'M HERE," and he adds "JUST LOOK UP!" At that moment I am reminded of a familiar scripture,

MATTHEW 28:20 "lo, I am with you always, even unto the end of the world". My eyes are open, and lights are off, light from the street shines through the window, I look upwards, and in an instant, I remember that right in the heart of my low place Jesus is right there waiting for me to just call his name! My help was waiting on me to call, and confess. Jesus then says to me... Nita I need you to sit up, and wake your husband up, and just like you cried out to me, do the same to him. I said, but he is asleep, he has to get early for work... Jesus immediately responds... this is his job do as I said and let him go to work... Christ reminds me of our vows. I'm up and i look towards my left again, and pat my husband on his back until he wakes up... and I say BABE...and he responded with "huh" ... I say I can't sleep!!! I'm afraid! Because of the diagnosis I have been given that I won't wake back up... I don't want to die like this!!! (Tears flood my face again) ... he gets up, and grabs me wrapping his arms around me, and his first 3 words are "DEAR HEAVENLY FATHER"... true intercessory prayer! When you follow God instructions your cry for help can be answered sooner than you think. As my husband talks, and petitions God, I could feel the weight lifting. I'm beginning to regain my strength. It took the action of obedience! My husband finishes, and says amen, he looks at me, and speaks a word that removes all doubt and fear. He reminds me that God has the final say. He awakens my memory of **PHILIPPIANS 4:13 "I can do all things through Christ which strengtheneth me"** ... he reassures me that I am ok... he then returns to his side of the bed... I lay back down, and close my eyes, and sleep then comes out of hiding.

A couple weeks go by, and I have a renewed look at life, and my health. I had to accept the diagnosis, and realize that it didn't mean it was the end of me. God had to reveal to me that I had to get to the root cause of my diagnosis, and that caused me to have to go back in time, and sift through my past. He showed me that the weight of my past was weighing me down. God boldly said to me, you must deal with this weight in order to handle your diagnosis. Even though I was prescribed certain medications for my situation, I learned that my true healing was not in the pills I was prescribed. It was in my obedience to God. Once I accepted what he said even though I thought I had dealt with my past... it was very clear that my past still had a hold on me.

Now I can say I am still here with improved health. I'm nearly a 100lb lighter, blood pressure regulated, blood sugar normal, and I no longer need an inhaler for asthma.

I say this with all the joy I can consume... that diagnosis did not change or affect my destiny. I shall have everything God promised me. It was, and is a process we all must go through with God to get to our destiny.

My process was from diagnosis to deliverance,
From deliverance headed towards my destiny.

Melanie Marie Hughes' story

I am the woman with the issue of blood. Since I was a child, I imagined having children, what it would feel like to be pregnant and to become a mother. Well my story was not the fairy tale I had imagined it to be. My nine months was cut short, and my miracle was born early because of my issue of blood.

I was diagnosed with preeclampsia (Pregnancy Induced Hypertension) or High Blood Pressure when pregnant, and it can be very dangerous because it can turn into eclampsia which will cause your organs to shut down fast and it could cause death. So, at 28 weeks the doctors said to me; we need to deliver your baby now or you and your baby might not make it. I was scared because I knew how early it was. So, I just prayed and declared the word over me, and my baby life. I said we shall live, and not die and declare the good works of the lord. My baby was born at 28 weeks old and her lungs were fully developed. It was truly a miracle.

I thought after delivering my baby my issue would go away, but that was far from the truth. I was in intensive care after giving birth because my blood pressure was extremely high. My body was so swollen I looked like two people, and I was very unbalanced. I was sent home on high blood pressure medicine. A year later, I was diagnosed with fibroids which caused me to bleed very heavily, and caused extreme pain during my period. Sometimes it would even cause problems during intercourse because it was so painful. Whenever it was that time of month, I would have anxiety because I knew at any time I would bleed out of my clothes. So now I have two issues of blood. I tried everything wearing two pads, and a tampon nothing worked. I had to keep a change of clothes with me. So, I dreaded that time of the month. Doctors wanted me take hormones, but I refused them because they're known to cause cancer. Cancer runs in my family, and I didn't want it, so for years I dealt with this issue. When I got pregnant with my second child it had gotten worse. So now I have not only fibroids but I also have cysts. My fibroids got bigger and I had one the size of a tennis ball inside of my uterus. I was able to carry my daughter full term at 38 weeks. I was in critical condition once again. My husband, and I decided that tying my tubes would be the best decision to make because every time I was pregnant, I was in critical condition. My husband said, he didn't want to take the chance of losing me. After tying my tubes, I started getting real bad cramps, and bleeding even heavier. I continued to pray my way through, and I was able to hold off on getting any surgeries until my daughter turned eight years old. By now the fibroids have attached themselves to my other organs, and my blood levels were low. I had to make a decision on how to handle this situation because it had gotten serious. The doctor offered me different options, and the one I chose was a partial hysterectomy. I was told there was a chance the fibroids would grow back. I went to the hospital for a one-day procedure only to stay two extra days because my bowels would not move. I was sent home to recover the third day. I got home and still didn't feel right. I went back to the emergency room, and the doctor took my blood only to find out my blood levels were low, and the doctor said that I might need a blood transfusion if my blood levels get any lower. My instructions were to contact my doctor immediately. I made an appointment with my doctor. My doctor examined me, and said it was normal to have low blood levels after the surgery I had. So, my husband took me home. I started to get really weak, lost my mobility and my stomach was hard like

I was carry an alien in my belly. I made another appointment. When I arrived at the appointment the doctors wanted to send me home again like nothing was wrong, but my husband decided to take me to the emergency room immediately disregarding everything the doctor said. When I got to the hospital there was a physician assistant that came in and looked at me and said Mrs. Hughes you don't look well so I'm going to send you to get a cat scan of your belly. I was so tired at this point. The physician assistant came back with the results, and he looked at me, and said Mrs. Hughes you're not crazy you have an infected hematoma and we need to send you back to the hospital by ambulance right away. Tears just ran down my face in relief because I already knew it was an issue of blood, and I was fighting for my life once again. I was admitted to the hospital, and they explained to me that my stomach was full of blood and it was infected. The center of disease control came in to try to figure out what type of bacteria it was. The doctors tried various kinds of antibiotics but they were running out of options and time. My family came to see me and prayed with me. I said to my aunt, I am like the women from the bible with the issue of blood. I said if I could grab hold to the hem of his garment, I would be made whole. I grabbed my aunts dress, a symbolization of Jesus garment I felt the presence of God in that hospital room. Doctors figured out what type issue I had purse my flesh to drain the blood and treated the infection. No matter what your issue of blood is, have faith, and God will take care of you. You are not alone; Do not be ashamed, tug on the hem of his garment, and be made whole. Pick up your cross and walk, proclaim that you shall live, and not die to declare the good works of the lord. God loves you. Amen

NNylari Iralynn's story

In 2005 the woman who was known as Iralynn Johnson died. The life I once knew was no longer available to me. There was no magic pill I could pop, and no physical therapy that could heal this. In my mind, I was now trapped inside of a body that produces nothing but chronic pain, headaches, muscle spasms, and sciatica down my legs.

I was angry with God when I found out I had a Degenerative Disc Disease in the cervical area of my back, and there was no cure. I remember walking away from Him, not wanting to sing for him, and just deciding to do everything I was big and bad enough to do. I felt like God was punishing me for nothing. I felt as if I had been trying my best to live right for so long at the age of 24, I attended church every Sunday, got married, I was faithful to my husband, took my child to church with me, and I sung in the choir, and I still had to deal with this thorn in my flesh. I felt like it wasn't far, and I didn't deserve this kind of hell.

It had been over 10 years of nonstop pain, and I was sick of me. Spiraling into a deep depression as I popped my narcotic medications, and muscle relaxers to numb the pain of standing too long, sitting too long, and holding my head up, I was in a very dark place in my mind. I was sick of crying, sick of the alter call, sick of living a life full of pain. Standing outside next to my car crying out to God, asking

Him to allow me to have just one day free of pain, promising never to pray this prayer again if He would just allow me to feel how I felt before I gave birth to my first child. I wanted to remember what it felt like to get a full night of rest, I wanted to remember what it felt like to not have to take several breaks throughout the day to lay down so my pain wouldn't increase.... I wanted to feel like me again. Not realizing that this was the new me, and I was grieving the death of the person I once was. I didn't want to embrace this new person, this new life, these new circumstances. I was preparing myself for my second death. I never knew I would have to grieve like this.

I had thought it all through and made up my mind that taking my own life would be much easier than barring this cross full of nonstop pain. I would take all of my pills at once, and go to sleep to never wake up to this painful hell hole called my life. But every time I had made up my mind about suicide, someone would always randomly stop by to visit me, call or text or one of my kids would come, and hug me so tight, and say, "I love you mommie." I knew it was God saving me from myself.

Smiling through my pain as I go about my day had become my normal. I was faking it to make it, but sometimes faking it didn't work. Some days I had to lay in bed, and cry all day until my pain levels reduced. God had to show me how to restore my heart, and mind, and focus on the new person He was creating me to be.

I was so broken inside but I had to go back to God, and ask for forgiveness for leaving His protecting arms. I didn't know how much this chronic illness would teach me about being compassionate towards others who are dealing with illnesses. I didn't know that I needed to be humbled, and taught how to truly seek God for everything I needed. Having Degenerative Disc Disease has shown me how to love, forgive, and press past how I feel on a daily basis. I believe that I am already healed spiritually and my physical routine is just necessary maintenance.

I am not the angry person the enemy wants me to be, God will help me shift my attitude and I will be better, and greater than I was on yesterday.

I am the loving person God wants me to be, and that love will shine through every time someone encounters me. I will show others Jesus Christ.

I am a daily overcomer because I renew my mind with the application of God's word.

Shifting my thought life

During a depressing moment I found myself having to tap into my God bank to push myself to fight when I didn't want to, to remember scriptures that ministered to me, and speak

them to myself until I believed them. Sometimes we have to fight our own mental state to cross the road, and be better.

I am everything God wants me to be. Depression doesn't own my mind, my emotions or my character. I take authority over it, and I overcome it every time because I know that God has a purpose, and he definitely has a plan for my life that will not be stopped by any negative thought the enemy tries to put in my mind. God's word will help me defeat the giants in my mind. I am healed in the spirit and my physical healing is on the way.

I am prepared for the battle, and I will not allow anything to get me off course. Every attack is null and void and dead on arrival because God has shown me how to change my atmosphere, and I will take action in the moment. (I am prepared with my bible in hand, positive music, writing materials, and art supplies to shift my thoughts back to a state of positivity).

Chapter 3
I will wait patiently on the Lord

I will wait patiently on the Lord

Psalm 40:1-3 ESV

I called to the Lord, and he heard me.
  He heard my cries.
² He lifted me out of the grave.
  He lifted me from that muddy place.
He picked me up, put me on solid ground,
  and kept my feet from slipping.
³ He put a new song in my mouth,
  a song of praise to our God.
Many will see what he did and worship him.
  They will put their trust in the Lord.

Affirmation

I will wait patiently

I am not fearful for my God is always covering me with His loving arms.

I am not nor will I be frustrated in or during the process, I will wait on the Lord.

I am worth more, and I cannot die until every dream, and purpose inside of me has been birthed.

I am allowing God to humble my spirit.
I am deserving of love, care, and respect. God provides this for me, and I will accept it.

I will wait patiently on the Lord

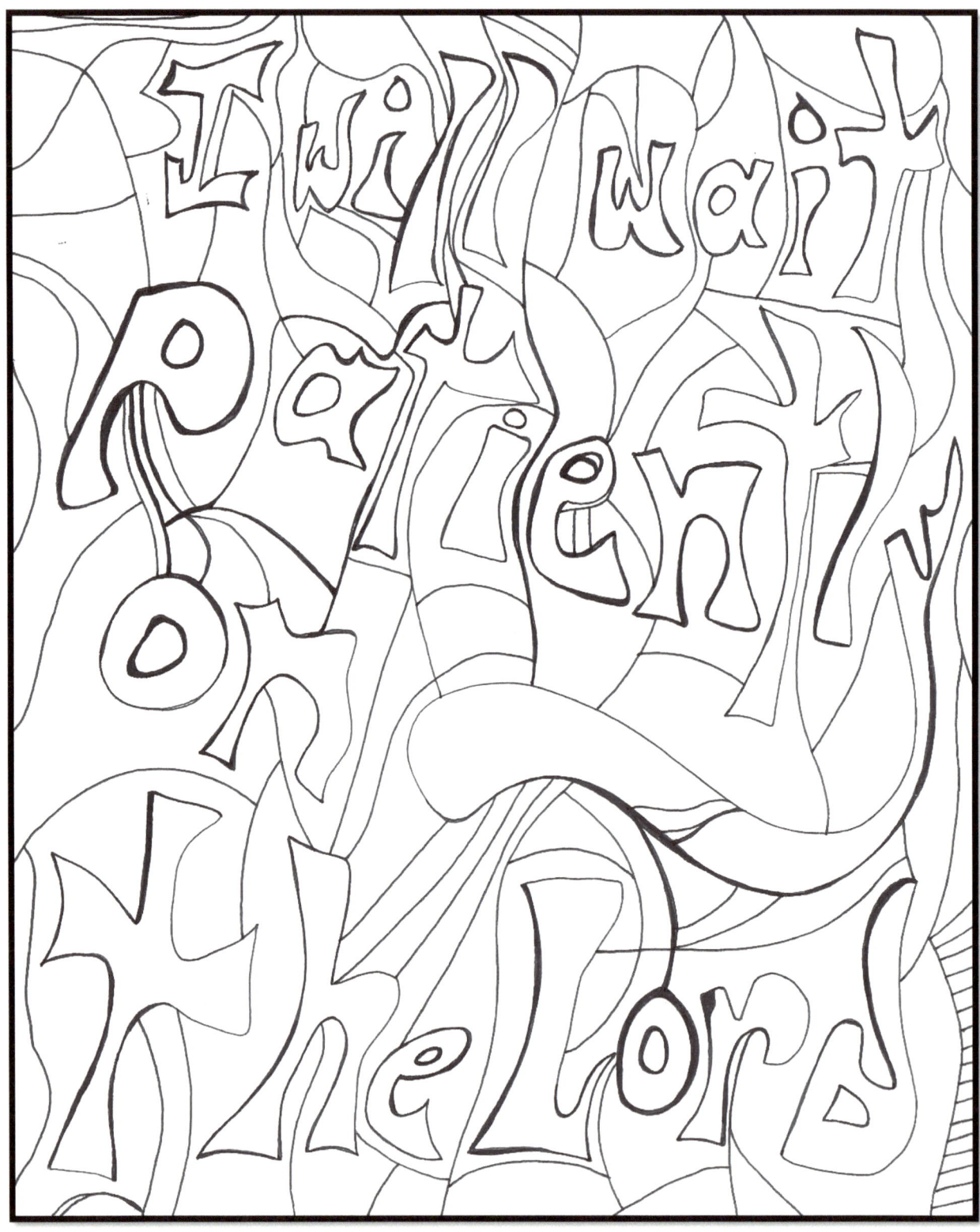

Notes/Reflections

Notes/Reflections (How did this affirmation and art work make you feel? Write, draw, color your response below.)

Chapter 4
God will strengthen and help me

God will strengthen and help me

Isaiah 41:10 NKJV

Fear not, for I *am* with you;
Be not dismayed, for I *am* your God.
I will strengthen you,
Yes, I will help you,
I will uphold you with My righteous right hand.

Affirmation

I am strong

I am motivated by the word of God, and I will speak positively over my life, my mind and my future.

I am strong in mind because of Jesus Christ and I will study to show myself approved.

I am the overcomer God created me to be and I will not allow life's struggles and challenges to shift my mind from this belief. God is raising me up to be one of His warriors and I will do it humbly.

I am strong enough to counteract every negative thought that comes to my mind and I will defeat it by continuously feeding my mind God's word on a daily basis, speaking what I believe, and applying it to my life.

-NNylari Iralynn

God will strengthen and help me

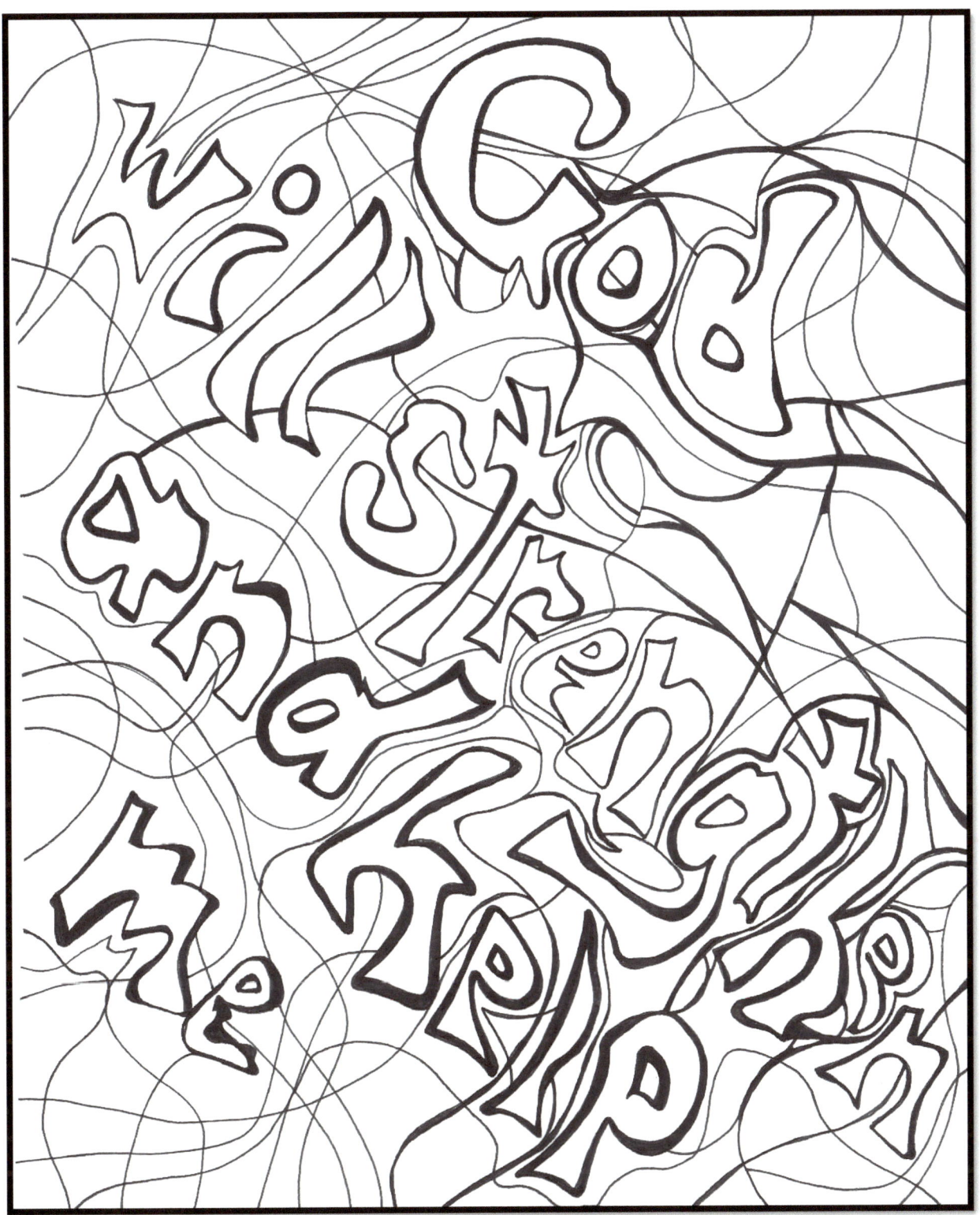

Notes/Reflections

Notes/Reflections (How did this affirmation and art work make you feel? Write, draw, color your response below.)

Chapter 5
I am not alone

I am not alone

Deuteronomy 31:8 NIV

⁸ The L<small>ORD</small> himself goes before you and will be with you; he will never leave you nor forsake you. Do not be afraid; do not be discouraged."

Affirmation

I am not alone

I will be open to new ideas, and ways to become a better me.

I am working on the challenging areas of my life, and applying God's word to fill every empty space.

I am open to talking about what I am feeling, and I will not push away the people in my life when I am experiencing a challenging moment in my mind. I will seek to be encouraged by the people God has places in my life to uplift me.

I am the unforgotten child of God. God has gone before me to make a way for me. The challenges I will face is only a necessary part of Gods development plan for me so that I can fulfill His purpose for my life like he desires me to do and I will have peace in the process.

-NNylari Iralynn

I am not alone

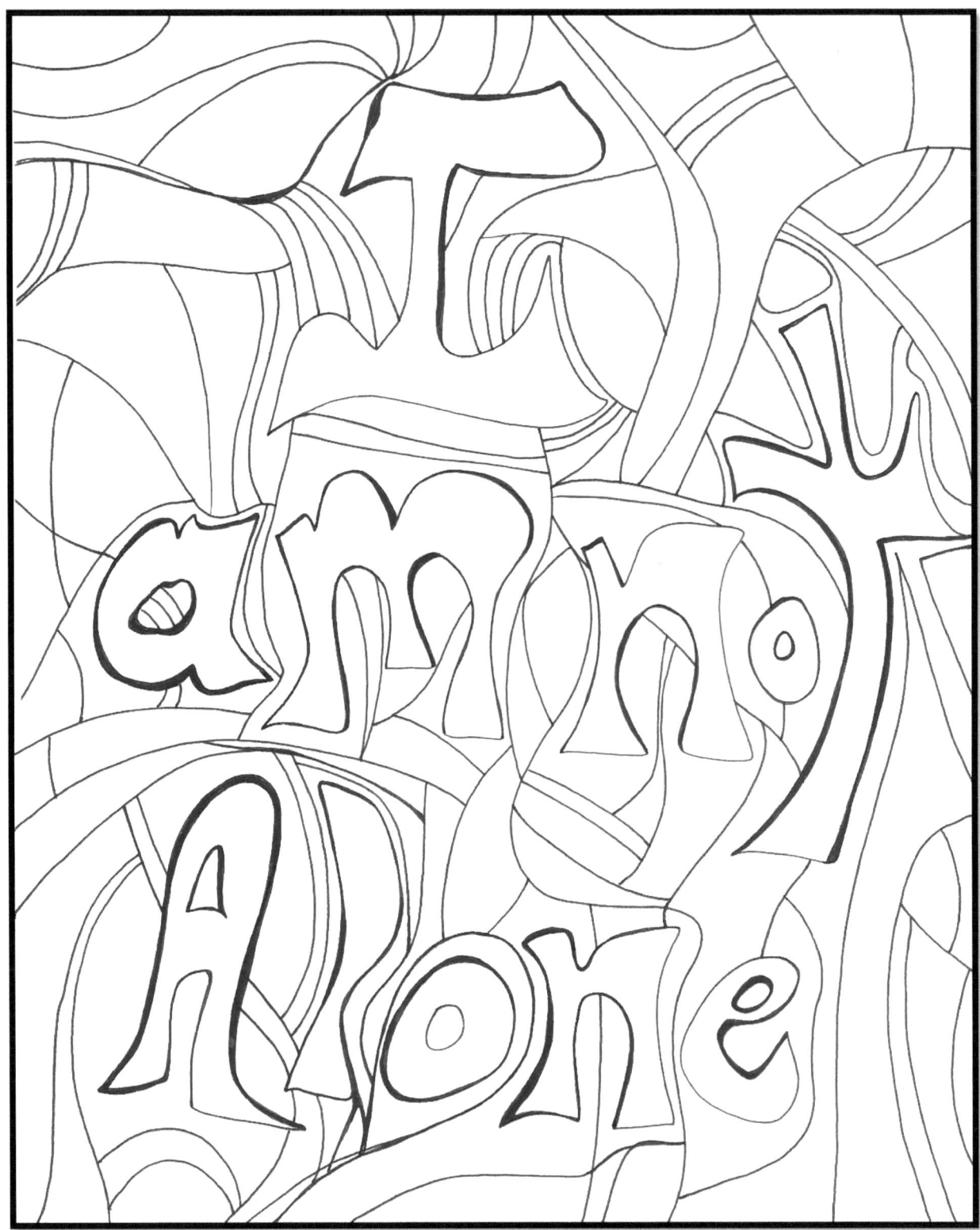

Notes/Reflections

Notes/Reflections (How did this affirmation and art work make you feel? Write, draw, color your response below.)

Chapter 6
I will put my hope in God

I will put my hope in God

Isaiah 40:31 NKJV

But those who wait on the LORD
Shall renew *their* strength;
They shall mount up with wings like eagles,
They shall run and not be weary,
They shall walk and not faint.

Affirmation

I will put my hope in God

I will wait on God

I will trust in God

I will make myself available to gain a clear understanding of who God is.

In getting this understanding, I will put my hope in God.

In return, I will grow, I will progress, and I will become better equipped to walk in my destiny.

I am who I am because God is who he is.

-Tonita Walker

I will put my hope in God

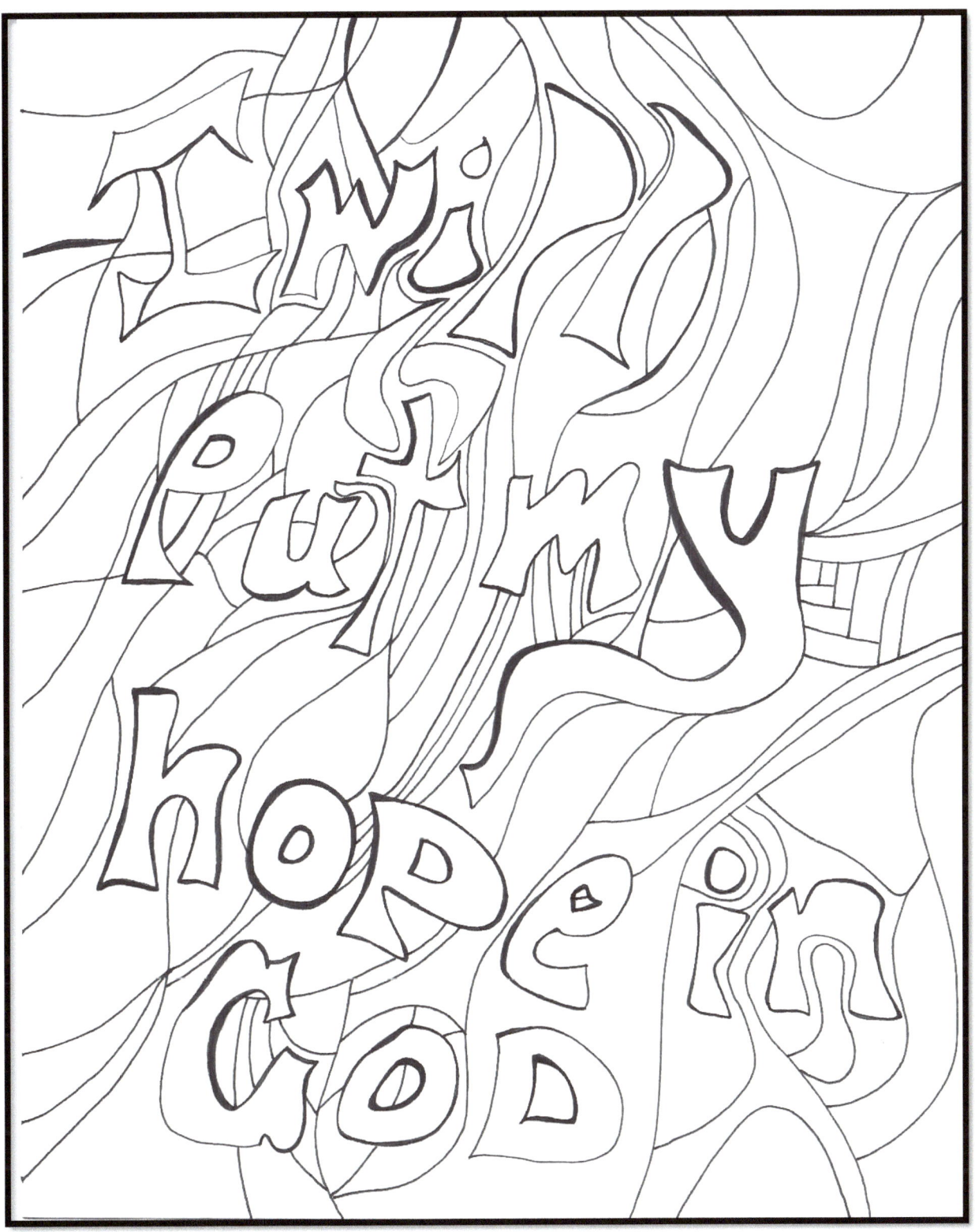

Notes/Reflections

Notes/Reflections (How did this affirmation and art work make you feel? Write, draw, color your response below.)

Chapter 7
God will take care of me

God will take care of me

1Peter 5:6-7 NKJV

Therefore, humble yourselves under the mighty hand of God, that He may exalt you in due time, [7] casting all your care upon Him, for He cares for you.

Affirmation

God will take care of me

I will humble myself, and do Gods will

I admire God, and respect who He is

I will be content with who I am being in a state of peaceful happiness with me!

God praises and respects the serenity of me

In my acceptance of whatever situation, I'm in, God will honor me, he will reward me.

I will hand over all my troubles, and concerns because God looks after me and provides for me.

-Tonita Walker

God will take care of me

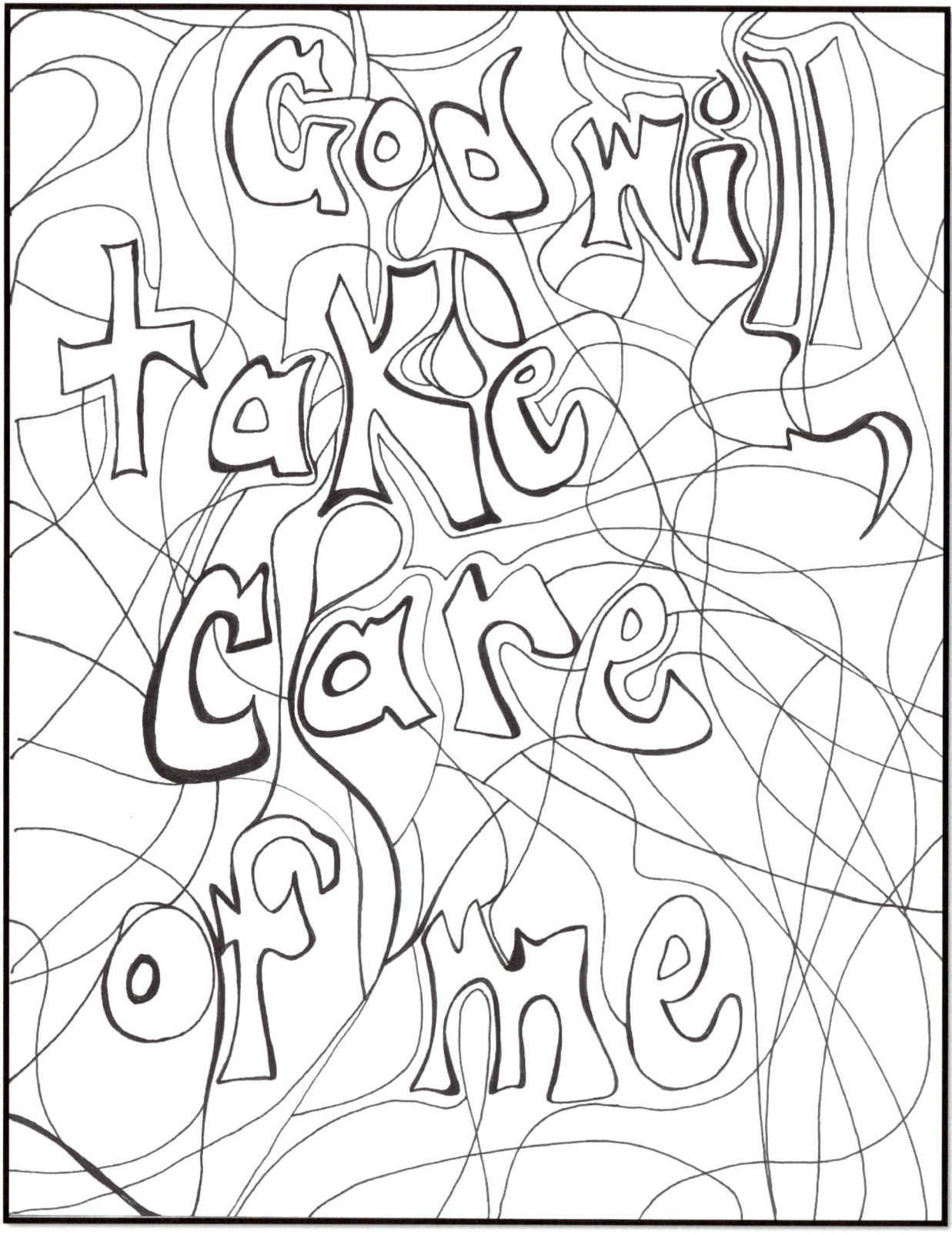

Notes/Reflections

Notes/Reflections (How did this affirmation and art work make you feel? Write, draw, color your response below.)

Chapter 8
God's Will Must Be Done

Finding hope in God

Isaiah 40:31(40:26-31)

To put your hope into something or someone, is the grounds for believing that something good may happen. Hope has the synonyms of confidence and faith. That is, one's belief that one can rely on someone. It is having a firm trust and a strong belief in God, based on spiritual apprehension rather than proof. God has already proven himself to be who he is. When you understand who God is, trusting him becomes easier. Understanding who God is, is when you grasp the fact that he is the Creator of all the earth, and He never grows weak or weary (Isaiah 40:28). In that fact you can truly see where your source of strength, and power comes from. This source of strength, and power cannot be activated until you put your trust in Him. If you know, and understand who the source is, you know where to put your hope. I put my hope in God because I know, and believe He is who He says He is. In Isaiah 45:5-12, God tells us exactly who He is. In verse twelve in the New Living Translation He says, "I am the one who made the earth, and created people to live on it. With my hands I stretched out the heavens. All the stars are at my command." I became me because of God. He created me, and everything I have access to. God is the head commander, and the ruler over all. I put my hope in what is effective, and what last. God is successful in producing my every need, want, and desire. All that I need is in him. In this stock market of life, I invest my hope, and I make a continuous profit of strength, and power. God said I can do all things if I do it through Him (Philippians 4:13). So, what are you investing, and who are you investing in?

It's Not About How You Feel

In our society today, everyone seems to be wrapped up with their own personal feelings, and because of those feelings they think that they can be who they want to be, do what they want to do, and act how they want to act. God's commands have become just another book on the shelf, another decorative piece in the room, or an old folk tale but never a direct order for our lives. We might pick up the bible, and read it, and study it but still refuse to apply it to our daily lives. It's times to make a tough decision, and follow God's commands. Doing God's will for your life doesn't require feelings, only obedience. You may be feeling pain all over your body or even have the urge to satisfy your fleshly desires to be with someone of the same sex, participate in fornication or adultery but we were not created to fulfill our own fleshly desires, we we're created to worship God, and fulfill His plan for our lives which means we cannot act on feelings, but only in obedience unto God. If you are a man, God's word says you are to leave your father, and mother and cleave unto your wife. The word also tells us that fornication is not right, and a man loving a man or woman loving a woman is an abomination. If God said that we are to follow His commandments, then that is what we are to do. We are not our own. We belong to God… We must remind ourselves of that daily.

Finding Joy in the Imperfect times

I have learned to find joy in the imperfect moments in my life. For in the imperfect moments there is always something I can learn, and share. Life is an uncomfortable story of how things are learned, shared, given, and taken. Some stories are heard, and seen as beautiful, but it depends on who's holding the mic, and the paint brush.

You may be asking; how do you find joy in the imperfect times... It starts by deciding that, that is what you are going to do, writing down a plan of action, and making the next step to just do it. It's not going to feel good the first, second or third time you do it but you just have to do it. Sometimes your joy won't come easy, so you have to fight for your joy. How do you fight for your joy? Ask God to go before you and empower you to fight, then you have to put in some work, but never give up! God is with you always, keep fighting.

Courage to do the Lords will despite daily suffering

Matthew 28:19-20

In the book of Matthew 28:19-20, Jesus told the disciples to "go ye therefore, and teach all nations, baptizing them in the name of the Father, and of the Son, and of Holy Ghost," it is not recorded as to whether or not the disciples gave Jesus a long list of reasons why they couldn't do what He asked. In fact, nothing was said in regards to the feelings of the disciples, and to me it speaks volumes on how we are to respond to what God is telling us to do in His name without stating the fact that we are sick, ill, or just don't want to do what He said to do. Jesus already knows that you have an illness, He already knows that you have chronic pain all over your body, but He is asking for your selfless obedience to His will for your life in spite of what you are feeling in your body. The Lord called you to do something great for His kingdom. Will you answer the call?

I am NNylari Iralynn, Renaissance woman

Tonita Walker

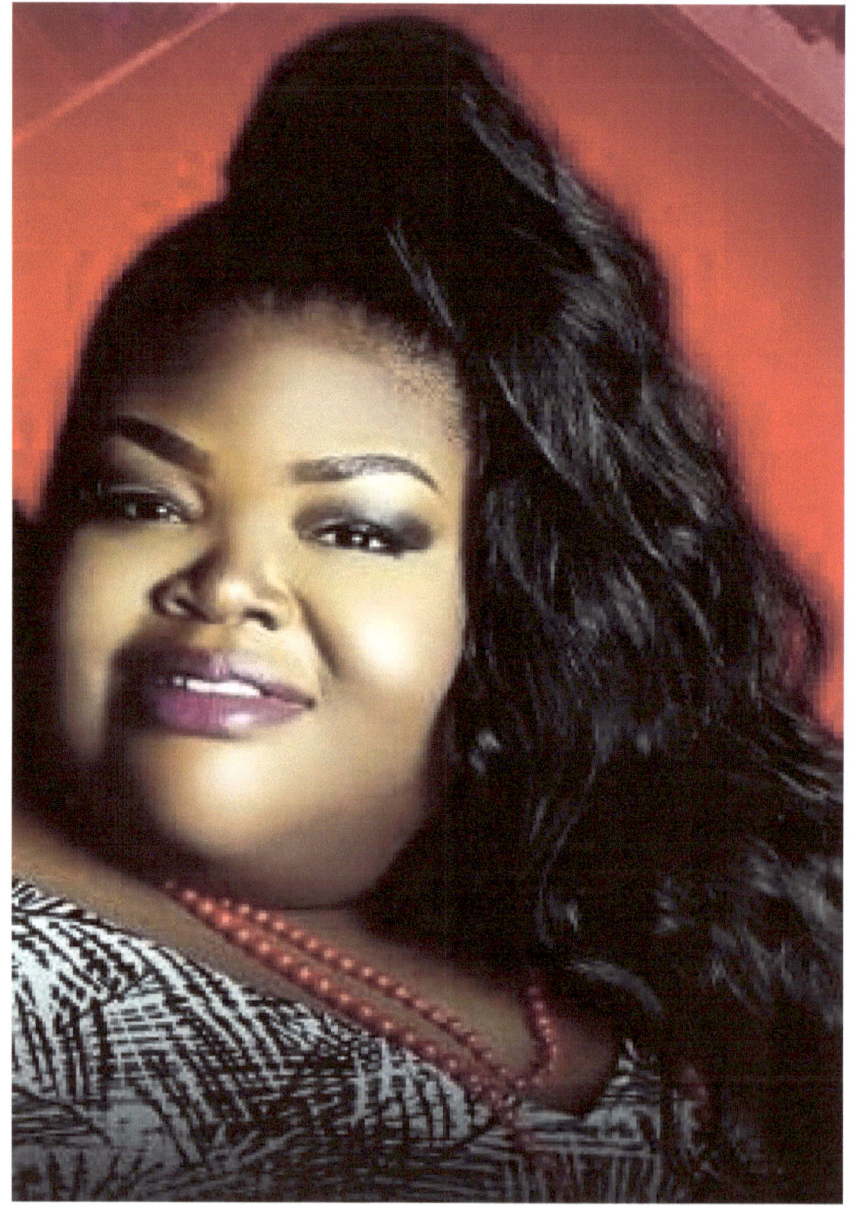

Website: www.tandimusic.com

Email: tonitajwalker@gmail.com

Social Media: @tonitajwalker @tandimusic

Melanie Marie Hughes

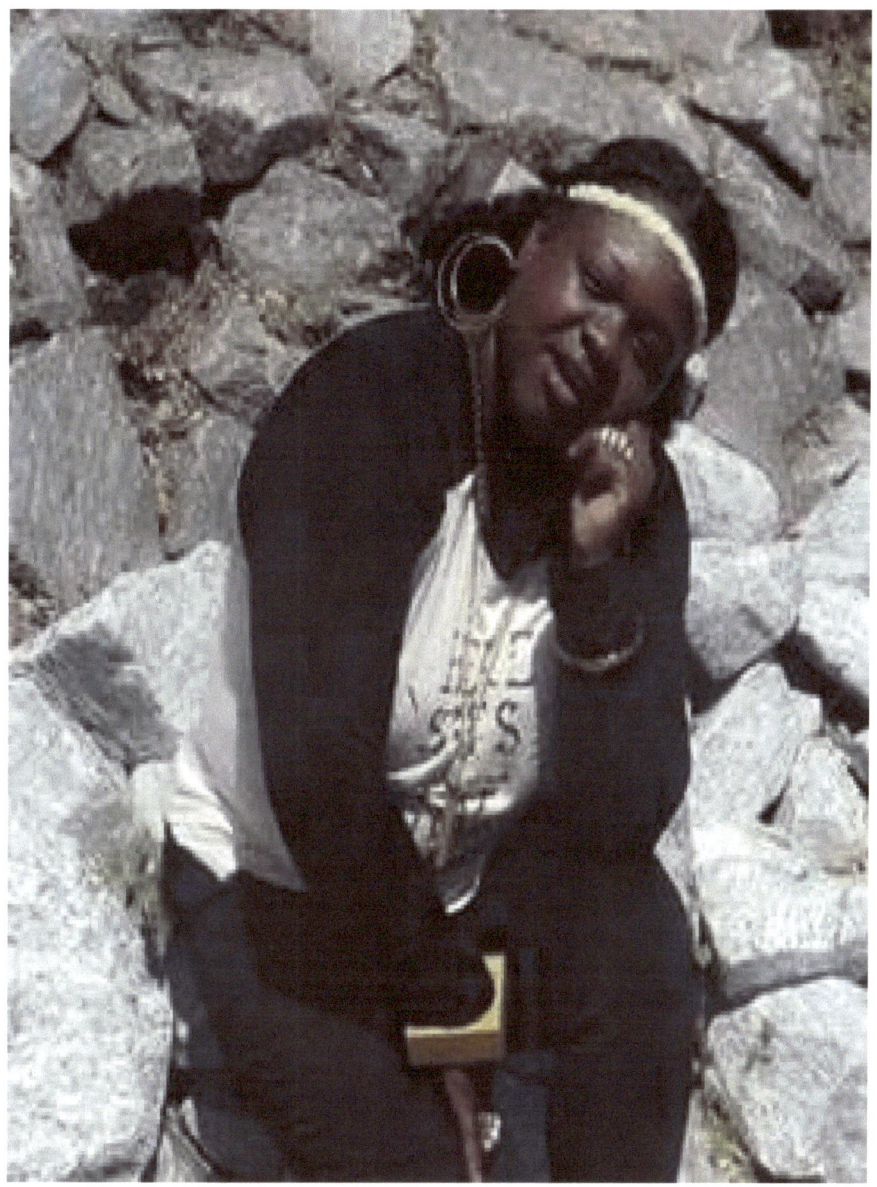

Email: mhmelaniehughes@gmail.com

Facebook @melaniehughes

Instagram @myhusbandnme2005

NNylari Iralynn

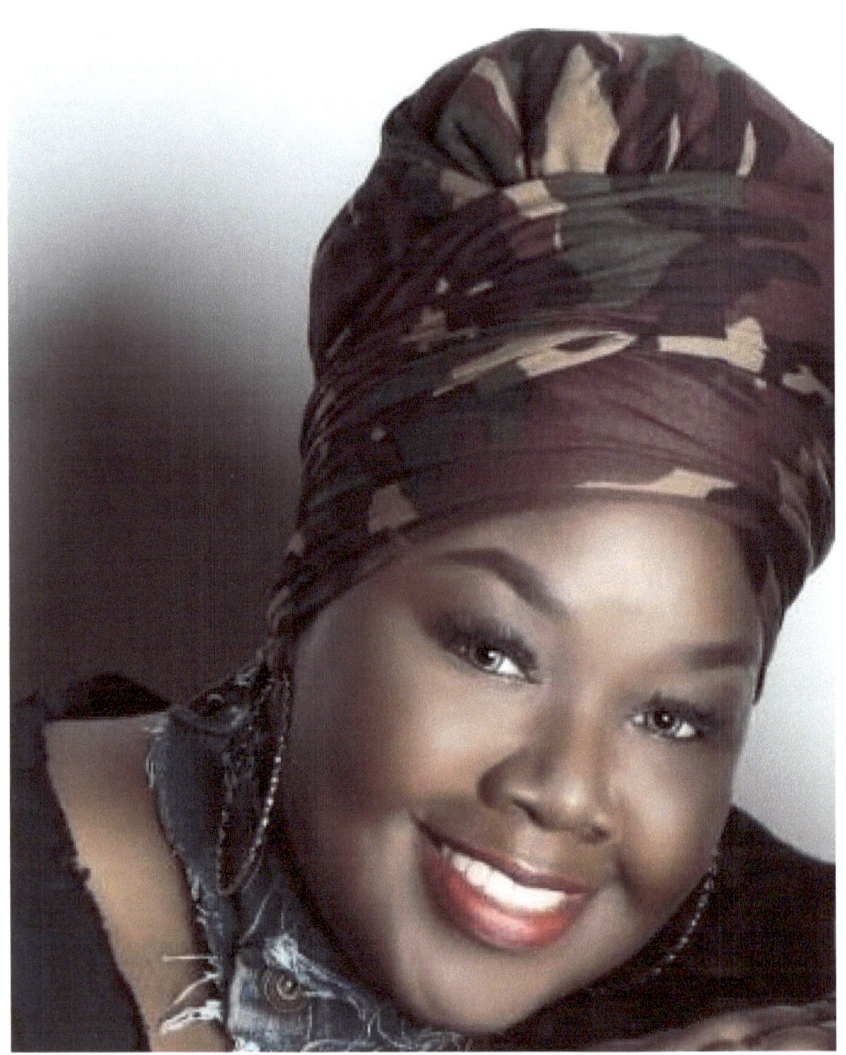

Website: www.nnylariiralynn.com

Website: www.tandimusic.com

Email: info@nnylariiralynn.com

Social Media: @nnylariiralynn @tandimusic

www.ingramcontent.com/pod-product-compliance
Lightning Source LLC
Chambersburg PA
CBHW051202220526
45473CB00003B/874